GRADE 5

Read and Remember

Individual and Group Activities
for Fiction and Nonfiction Reading

AUTHORS ☺☺

Mandy Lohman
and
Erin Richardson

Carson-Dellosa Publishing Company, Inc.
Greensboro, North Carolina

DEDICATION

This series is dedicated to Chris Lohman and Kevin Richardson for their continued support and encouragement throughout this project.

Credits

Editor
Tara Poitras

Layout Design
Jon Nawrocik

Illustrations
Ray Lambert

Cover Design
Peggy Jackson

Printed in the USA
All rights reserved.
ISBN 0-88724-943-4

Table of Contents

Introduction

Help students read **and** remember! The creative activities in this book were designed to improve students' reading comprehension skills—by addressing one story element at a time.

To help students focus on each story detail, activities are divided into four sections: Character, Setting, Plot, and Overall Story.

Activities for both fiction and nonfiction selections are included in each section. The activities can be completed by individual students, with partners, or by small groups. A quick visual reference is included at the bottom of each page to help teachers and students choose an appropriate activity. See the examples to the left.

Teachers can make packets of various activities for each student. Or, the activities can be used in a reading center, where students choose an activity to complete after they have read a fiction or nonfiction selection. During reading-group time, teachers can work with a small group of students to complete an activity. Advanced students that need to be challenged with independent work will also benefit from completing these activities.

Activity instructions ("What You Do") address the student. They can be photocopied for students to read themselves, or the teacher can give verbal instructions. A materials list ("What You Need") is included for each activity. Items are listed in the order students will use them. Some activities also include "Supplies You Could Use," a list of additional materials students might use to complete an activity.

Most activities include a "Note to the Teacher." This section includes any specific directions for the teacher, plus options for completing the activity.

FICTION ☺

This individual activity (☺) can be used with a fiction selection.

NONFICTION ☺ ☺

This small-group or partner activity (☺ ☺) can be used with a nonfiction selection.

Rapigzell! Rapigzell! Let down your golden pigtail.

Master List of Materials

What You Need:

beans
cassette recorder (optional)
cassette tape (optional)
chart paper
clothing
colored pencils
construction paper
copy paper (legal-sized)
crayons
dictionary
glue
highlighter
hot glue (optional)
index cards (4" x 6")
markers
notebook paper
paint
paintbrush
papier-mâché
pencil (or pen)
plastic mask
poster board
props
rice
scissors
seeds
shoe boxes (2)
stapler
thesaurus
video camera (optional)
videotape (optional)
white glue
white paper
yardstick

Supplies You Could Use:

beads
colored paper
craft foam
craft sticks
felt
masking tape
plastic foam
putty
string or yarn
toys (small)

LIVING MUSEUM

What You Do:

1. "Become" a character from a book you have read.

2. Complete the Living Museum Activity Sheet. If needed, find additional information about the character by reading other books, searching the Internet, viewing videos, etc. Write the book title and author's name on the back of the activity sheet.

3. Find clothing and props appropriate for your character.

4. Write a script that describes the character and some of the events in which he was involved. Then, memorize your script.

5. Dress up as your character and recite your script to the class.

Notes to the Teacher:
- You can have one or two students perform each day or have the whole class perform and invite other classes to watch.

- You could also arrange a performance for parents to visit and view your classroom's "living museum."

What You Need:
LIVING MUSEUM ACTIVITY SHEET

PENCIL (OR PEN)

CLOTHING AND PROPS

NOTEBOOK PAPER

Living Museum Activity Sheet

Your name _____

Character's name _____

Date of birth _____ Date of death _____

Birthplace _____

Career _____

Family members _____

Why did you choose this character? _____

_____

_____

Interesting fact #1 _____

_____

_____

Interesting fact #2 _____

_____

_____

Interesting fact #3 _____

_____

_____

Interesting fact #4 _____

_____

_____

Life Links

What You Do:

1. Make chain links to display important facts about a character from a book you have read.

2. Complete the Life Links Templates. If needed, read other books or search the Internet to find additional information. Write another important detail about the character's life on the blank chain on template #2.

3. Cut the links apart.

4. Write the book title, author's name, and your name on the back of the link with the character's name. Then, staple the chain link to form a circle.

5. Loop the birth date link through the first chain and staple the ends to form the second link.

6. Repeat step #5 with the remaining links to complete the chain.

What You Need:

Life Links Templates

pencil (or pen)

scissors

stapler

Life Links Template #1

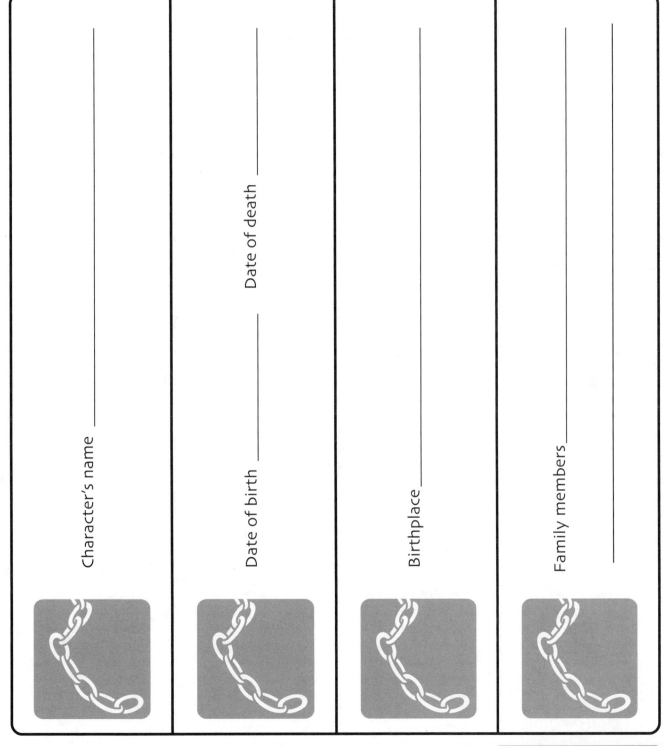

Character's name _____

Date of death _____

Date of birth _____

Birthplace _____

Family members _____

Life Links Template #2

How was this person important in the book?

How did the actions of this person affect the lives of others?

Why did you choose this person?

Acrostic Poem

What You Do:

1. Write an acrostic poem about a character from a book you and a partner have read.

2. On a sheet of paper, write the character's name horizontally. This will be the title.

3. Write the character's name vertically in uppercase letters, along the left side of the paper.

4. With your partner, brainstorm ideas that could be included in the poem.

5. Beside each letter, write short phrases that describe the character. Each phrase should begin with the letter that begins the line. See the example poem below.

   Lincoln
   L ived in Illinois
   I s on the penny
   N ominated for president in 1860
   C ivil War president
   O pposed to slavery
   L eader of the Union
   N ever gave up on his people

What You Need:
notebook paper
pencil (or pen)
construction paper
markers or
colored pencils

6. Rewrite the poem on a sheet of construction paper. Use markers or colored pencils to write the character's name vertically in uppercase letters, along the left side of the paper.

7. Draw and color a border around the poem using an idea that was presented in the poem. For example, the border for the acrostic poem about Lincoln could include pennies, a picture of Lincoln's face, etc.

8. Write the book title, author's name, your name, and your partner's name on the back of the poem.

Note to the Teacher:
Assign students to read a book with a partner.

Character Description

What You Do:

1. Describe a character from a book you have read.

2. Complete the top part of Description Activity Sheet #1.

3. Write four adjectives that describe the character.

4. Look up the adjectives in a thesaurus and write five synonyms for each word.

5. Complete the top part of activity sheet #2.

6. Write the adjectives again. Then, use each adjective to write a sentence that describes the character.

Note to the Teacher:
If desired, students can also write antonyms for each adjective on the back of activity sheet #1.

What You Need:

Description Activity Sheets

pencil (or pen)

thesaurus

Brave

Brave:
courageous
fearless
stalwart
valiant
intrepid
gallant
daring

Description Activity Sheet #1

Your name _____

Title _____

Author _____

Character's name _____

Adjectives	Synonyms
1. _____	_____
2. _____	_____
3. _____	_____
4. _____	_____

Description Activity Sheet #2

Your name _____

Title _____

Author _____

Character's name _____

Adjectives	Sentences
1. _____	_____
2. _____	_____
3. _____	_____
4. _____	_____

POINT OF VIEW

What You Do:

1. Using a different character's point of view, retell a chapter of a book you have read.

2. Use details and characteristics about this character's life, interests, hobbies, and any other information given in the book to rewrite the chapter from her perspective.

3. Brainstorm ideas for the new chapter. Think about how the new character would feel about the events and/or problems that occurred in the chapter.

4. Write the chapter from this new point of view on one or more sheets of notebook paper. Remember to include the book title, author's name, and your name on the paper.

Note to the Teacher:
If several students have read the same book, each student should select a different character to retell the chapter. When students have completed their chapters, you can gather them and make a class book.

What You Need:
notebook paper
pencil (or pen)

MASK

What You Do:

1. Use descriptive details and your imagination to make a mask of a character from a book you have read.

2. Start with a preformed plastic mask and make adjustments to it as needed. For example, you may need to use plastic foam, masking tape, or putty to change or enlarge the nose, cheeks, etc.

3. Use papier-mâché to cover the entire mask.

4. When the papier-mâché has dried, paint the mask. Then, add hair and any appropriate accessories to the mask. Some supplies you could use are listed below.

5. Write the book title, author's name, character's name, and your name on the Mask Activity Sheet. Then, write a description of the character from the character's point of view.

Supplies You Could Use:

beads	markers
colored paper	masking tape
craft foam	plastic foam
felt	putty
glue	yarn

Note to the Teacher:
If desired, students can choose characters from the same book. If so, students could also write a script and act out the story or part of the story after they have completed their masks.

What You Need:

preformed plastic mask

papier-mâché

paint

paintbrush

Mask Activity Sheet

pencil (or pen)

notebook paper (optional)

Mask Activity Sheet

Your name _____

Title _____

Author _____

Character's name _____

Character description _____

_____

_____

_____

_____

_____

_____

_____

_____

Career Research

What You need:

Career Research
Activity Sheet

pencil (or pen)

notebook paper

clothing and props
(optional)

What You Do:

1. Learn more about a character's career after you have read about it in a book.

2. Use the information you read in the book to brainstorm questions you would like to ask a person currently working in the profession you chose. You could also research the career by reading other books and searching the Internet.

3. Write six questions on the Career Research Activity Sheet. Complete the rest of the sheet.

4. Set up an appointment to meet with the person or speak with him on the phone. If you do not know anyone in the profession, ask your teacher to help you find someone to interview.

5. Ask your questions and record the person's answers on the activity sheet.

6. On a separate sheet of paper, explain why you chose this profession. You could include information from the book, any additional research you did, and the interview. You might also include quotes from the interview.

Note to the Teacher:
The career information gathered during this activity can be used in a job fair, where each student presents the information she learned about a profession to the rest of the class. Each student can dress up as a person in the profession she chose and have props to show as part of her presentation.

Career Research Activity Sheet

Career _____

Person being interviewed _____

Interviewer's name _____

Question 1 _____

_____

Answer _____

_____

Question 2 _____

_____

Answer _____

_____

Question 3 _____

_____

Answer _____

_____

Question 4 _____

_____

Answer _____

_____

Question 5 _____

_____

Answer _____

_____

Question 6 _____

_____

Answer _____

_____

SHADOW BOX

What You Do:

1. Make a shadow box to depict the setting of a book you have read.

2. Cut a hole about the size of a quarter in the middle of one end of a shoe box.

3. Use various materials in your classroom to create a three-dimensional scene inside the box. The scene should face the end of the box with the hole. Some supplies you could use are listed below.

4. Use a pencil or pen to create ten to fifteen small holes in the lid of the shoe box.

5. Complete the information on the Shadow Box Activity Sheet.

6. Cut out the activity sheet and glue it to the bottom of the shoe box.

7. Put the lid on the shoe box and look through the hole to see your three-dimensional scene.

Supplies You Could Use:

beads	felt
colored paper	poster board
construction paper	small toys
craft sticks	string or yarn

What You Need:

shoe box

scissors

glue

markers, crayons, colored pencils

pencil (or pen)

Shadow Box Activity Sheet

Shadow Box Activity Sheet

Shadow box designed by _____

Title _____

Author _____

Description of setting _____

_____

_____

_____

_____

_____

_____

_____

_____

Travel Brochure

What You Do:

1. Create a travel brochure based on the setting of a book your group has read.

2. Brainstorm ideas with your group. Record the information on a sheet of notebook paper. Include "Places to Go" and "Things to See and Do."

3. Edit the information with your group. Create the brochure using the Travel Brochure Templates.

4. Draw and color a picture on the front cover on template #1. The picture can be a scene from the book, part of the setting, etc.

5. Write your name and the names of the classmates in your group on the bottom of the front cover.

6. Write the information for "Places to Go" and "Things to See and Do" on template #2.

7. Draw and color a picture of the setting under "A Beautiful View." Write a caption for the picture in the box.

8. Cut out the brochure and fold it on the dashed line.

9. Write the book title and author's name on the back of the brochure.

Notes to the Teacher:

- Assign students to small groups to read a book together.

- Make double-sided copies of the template so that students can make their brochures easily.

What You Need:
pencil (or pen)

notebook paper

Travel Brochure Templates

markers, colored pencils

scissors

Travel Brochure Template #1

Travel to a Magical Place

Title _____

_____

_____

Author _____

_____

By:

Travel Brochure Template #2

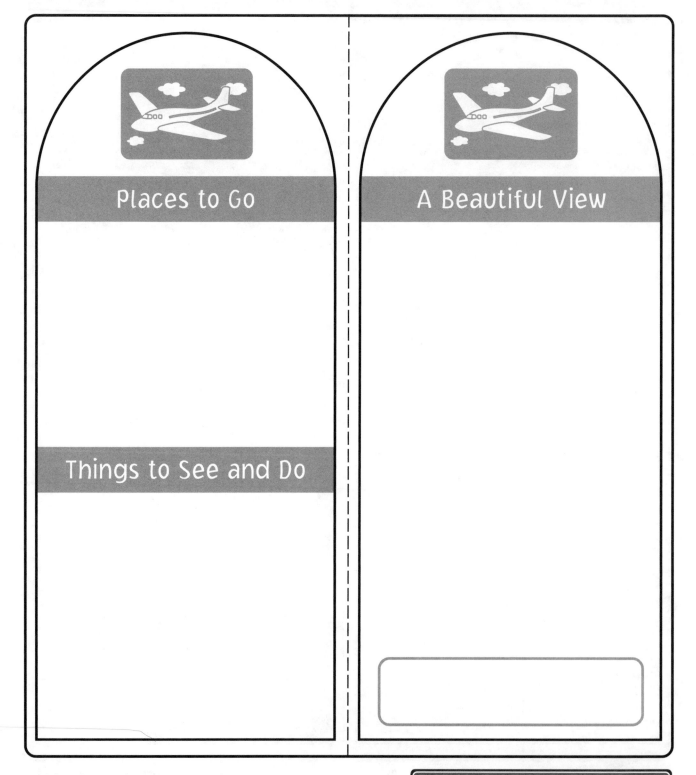

Places to Go

Things to See and Do

A Beautiful View

Catalog

What You Do:

1. Make a catalog of things to "sell" from a book your group has read.

2. With your group, select items and places from the setting to include in your catalog.

3. Write the name of each item or place on the Catalog Templates. Then, determine a price for each one and record it on the template.

4. Write a description of each item or place. Be creative when writing the descriptions. Then, draw and color a picture of each one.

5. Think of a creative name for the catalog and write it in the box on the cover on template #2. Write the book title, author's name, your name, and the names of the classmates in your group under the picture.

6. Cut out the template pages and staple them together to form the catalog.

Note to the Teacher:
Assign students to small groups to read a book together.

What You Need:

pencil (or pen)

Catalog Templates

markers, colored pencils, crayons

scissors

stapler

SLIGHTLY USED SHIP. CHEAP!

SUPPLIES $ $ $

ISLAND FOR SALE MAKE AN OFFER!

CRAZY CRUSOE'S BEACH SALE

Catalog Template #1

Item _____

_____

Price _____

Description _____

_____

_____

Item _____

_____

Price _____

Description _____

_____

_____

Catalog Template #2

Item _____

_____

Price _____

Description _____

_____

_____

Title _____

Author _____

Names _____

Mosaic Box

What You Do:

1. Create a mosaic box to capture elements from the setting of a book you have read.

2. Cut a sheet of white paper so that it is the same size as a shoe-box lid.

3. Draw a picture of the setting on the paper. Do not include too many details because the picture will be covered with beans, seeds, and rice.

4. Glue the drawing to the shoe-box lid.

5. Glue beans, seeds, and rice to the outline of the picture. Then, use them to fill in the picture.

6. Complete the information on the Mosaic Box Template. Cut apart the two sections and glue them to the sides of the shoe box.

7. On another sheet of white paper, draw and color several pictures of important items from the setting.

8. Cut the pictures apart and place them in your mosaic box.

What You need:

white paper

scissors

shoe box

pencil (or pen)

white glue

beans, rice, and seeds

hot glue (optional)

Mosaic Box Template

markers, crayons, colored pencils

Mosaic Box Template

Display designed by _____

Title _____

Author _____

Description of the setting _____

_____

_____

_____

_____

COMMERCIAL

What You Do:

1. Make a commercial for a book your group has read.

2. Use the plot of the book to create a commercial that will persuade others to read the book.

3. Brainstorm with your group the ideas you would like to include in the commercial.

4. Use the Commercial Activity Sheet as a rough draft for your ideas. Draw and color pictures in the boxes that correspond with the main events. Write the script on the lines below the boxes. Use additional copies of the activity sheet if needed.

5. Create the final project in one of the following ways:

   - Recreate the pictures and text on large pieces of poster board.
   - Record the commercial using a video camera.
   - Act out the commercial with the members of your group.
   - Produce a radio commercial using a cassette recorder.

Notes to the Teacher:
- Assign students to small groups to read a book together.

- Make enough copies of the activity sheet so that students can complete their commercials.

What You Need:
COMMERCIAL ACTIVITY SHEET
PENCIL (OR PEN)
MARKERS, COLORED PENCILS
POSTER BOARD (OPTIONAL)
VIDEO CAMERA (OPTIONAL)
CASSETTE RECORDER (OPTIONAL)

Commercial Activity Sheet

Commercial for _____

Weekly Planner

What You Do:

1. Create a weekly planner for the main character of a book you have read.

2. Write the character's name at the top of the Weekly Planner Template.

3. Use the main events from the book and your imagination to write appointments, events, reminders, etc., for the character each day.

4. Write the book title and author's name under "Notes." Write your name at the top of the page.

5. Cut out the page and fold it in half. Use white paper or construction paper to create a cover. Draw and color pictures on it to match the book.

Note to the Teacher:
If desired, students can make a planner page for each chapter in their books.

What You Need:
Weekly Planner Template

pencil (or pen)

scissors

construction paper or white paper

markers, crayons, colored pencils

Ye Olde Weekly Planner mon.

SLAY DRAGON 2:00

Weekly Planner Template

Name

Thursday

Friday

Saturday

Notes

Weekly planner for

Sunday

Monday

Tuesday

Wednesday

Timeline of Events

What You Do:

1. Plot the events of a chapter book as you are reading it with your group.

2. Write the book title and author's name across the top of a piece of poster board.

3. Use a yardstick to draw a line across the middle of the board.

4. After your group has read the first chapter, label the timeline with the chapter number or title and record the main event(s) that occurred.

5. Add to the timeline after you read each chapter.

6. Draw and color pictures on the poster board to match the information from the book.

7. Write your name and the names of the classmates in your group on the bottom of the poster board.

Note to the Teacher:
Assign students to small groups to read a book together.

What You need:
poster board

pencil (or pen)

yardstick

markers

Line

Bulletin Board

What You Do:

1. Create an informational bulletin board about a character or topic from a book your group has read. For example, you could create a bulletin board about Abraham Lincoln or alligators.

2. Brainstorm with your group the ideas you would like to include on the bulletin board.

3. Fold ten to twelve index cards in half. On the front of each card, write a question about a fact you learned about the person or topic. Write the question so that the fold of the card is on top.

   For example, Who was Abraham Lincoln's wife?
   Or, What type of water do alligators live in?

4. Write the answer to each question on the inside of the card.

5. On a sheet of paper, draw and color a picture to correspond with each question. Be sure the picture does not give away the answer to the question.

6. Staple the pictures and cards next to each other on the bulletin board.

7. Use construction paper to create a title for the bulletin board.

Notes to the Teacher:

- Assign students to small groups to read a book together.

- If a bulletin board is not available, the students can staple their cards and pictures to pieces of chart paper or poster board.

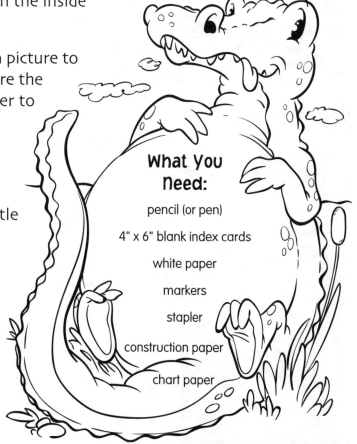

What You Need:

pencil (or pen)

4" x 6" blank index cards

white paper

markers

stapler

construction paper

chart paper

Book Glossary

What You Do:

1. Create a glossary for a book you are reading.

2. On a sheet of notebook paper, start a list of important words or terms from the book and add to it as you read.

3. Create the glossary using the Book Glossary Activity Sheet. Be sure to write the words in alphabetical order.

4. Include the pronunciation and definition for each word in your glossary. Use a dictionary as a reference to help you format your glossary.

5. Write the book title, author's name, and your name on the activity sheet.

Note to the Teacher:
If desired, students can complete this activity as they prepare for a test on nonfiction material.

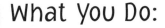

What You Need:

pencil (or pen)

notebook paper

Book Glossary Activity Sheet

dictionary

Book Glossary Activity Sheet

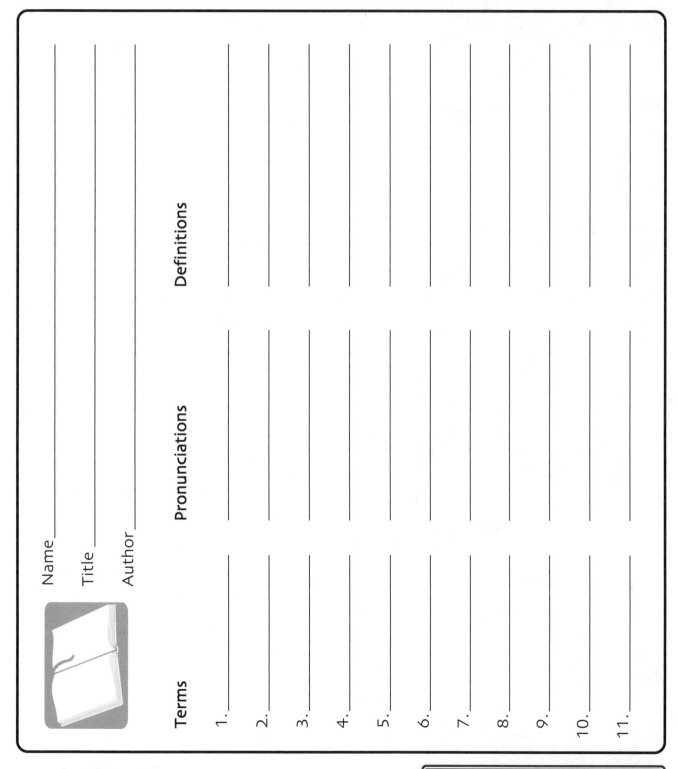

Name _____

Title _____

Author _____

Terms   **Pronunciations**   **Definitions**

1.
2.
3.
4.
5.
6.
7.
8.
9.
10.
11.

Chapter Performance

What You Do:

1. Act out a chapter from a book your group has read.

2. Choose characters and a narrator. Then, work together as a group to complete the Performance Activity Sheet.

3. Under "Cast," list the characters in the chapter and the name of the student portraying each character. The narrator should also be listed with the cast.

4. Write a narrative summarizing the chapter. Use the back of the activity sheet if you need more space.

5. Practice acting out the chapter as the narrator reads the narrative.

6. Perform the chapter for the rest of the class.

Notes to the Teacher:

- Assign students to small groups to read a book together.

- Each student should pick (or be assigned) a character from the chapter to portray.

- Students can bring in costumes and/or props for their performances.

What You Need:

pencil (or pen)

Performance Activity Sheet

costumes (optional)

props (optional)

Performance Activity Sheet

Title _____

Author _____

Chapter title _____

Cast

_____ played by _____

_____ played by _____

_____ played by _____

_____ played by _____

_____ played by _____

_____ played by _____

Narrative of chapter _____

_____

_____

_____

_____

_____

_____

CHAPTER OUTLINE

What You Do:

1. Outline a chapter from a book you have read.

2. Write the book title and author's name on the Chapter Outline Activity Sheet.

3. Write the chapter title or number as the main heading of the outline.

4. Write three or four main topics (I, II, III, and IV) under the title.

5. Under each topic, write three or four facts or details about the topic (A, B, C, and D). See the example below.

   Chapter 1: Snakes
   I. Snake senses
       A. Sight: This sense is not as developed as its other senses, but a snake can see things move.
       B. Smell: This is one of the snake's most powerful senses. A snake smells with its forked tongue.
       C. Hearing: A snake has no external ears. It "hears" by sensing vibrations through its jawbone.

6. Write your name on the back of the activity sheet.

Note to the Teacher:
You can also have students outline more than one chapter or all of the chapters from their books.

What You Need:
CHAPTER OUTLINE
ACTIVITY SHEET

PENCIL (OR PEN)

Chapter Outline Activity Sheet

Chapter
I._____
  A._____
II._____
  A._____
III._____
  A._____

Title _____

Author _____

Chapter title _____

I. _____

  A. _____

  B. _____

  C. _____

  D. _____

II. _____

  A. _____

  B. _____

  C. _____

  D. _____

III. _____

  A. _____

  B. _____

  C. _____

  D. _____

IV. _____

  A. _____

  B. _____

  C. _____

  D. _____

Class Paper

What You Do:

1. Make a newspaper about a time period in history or a country after your group has studied or read a book about it.

2. Using the book you have read, other books, and the Internet, gather information appropriate for your group's section of the newspaper.

3. Work with your group to write and edit an article about your topic. Type the final draft of the article on a computer and print it out.

4. Draw and color pictures or photocopy pictures for the article.

5. Fold sheets of legal-sized copy paper in half to look like a newspaper.

6. As a class, create a title and table of contents for the paper on a computer and print them out.

7. Lay out the title, table of contents, articles, and pictures on the legal paper. Then, glue the items to the sheets to create your class newspaper.

Notes to the Teacher:

- Assign students to small groups to create different sections of a newspaper. You could include:

Culture/Entertainment	Food
Current Events	Holidays/Festivals
Education	Sports
Fashion	

- If desired, the class newspaper could be created on a computer.

What You Need:

pencil (or pen)

notebook paper

white paper

markers, colored pencils

legal-sized copy paper

scissors

glue

EXTRA! EXTRA!

Journal of Chapters

What You Do:

1. Keep a journal to record the important events from a book you are reading.

2. Gather two sheets of notebook paper for each chapter.

3. Fold a sheet of construction paper in half. This will be the journal cover. Decorate the cover with a picture of the book's setting.

4. Place the sheets of notebook paper inside the cover. Staple the papers and cover together to form the journal.

5. Write a journal entry after you have read the first chapter. The entry should include the characters, main events, and the setting of the chapter. Be sure to label each entry with the title or number of the chapter.

6. Repeat step #5 for all of the chapters in the book.

Note to the Teacher:
Sheets of white paper may be included with the notebook paper so that students can draw and color pictures in their journals.

What You Need:
notebook paper
12" x 18" construction paper
pencil (or pen)
markers, crayons
colored pencils
stapler
white paper (optional)

GROG'S JOURNAL

Crossword Puzzle

What You Do:

1. Create a crossword puzzle about a book you have read.

2. On a sheet of notebook paper, make a list of clues or questions about the book. Write a total of ten clues: five clues across and five clues down.

3. Write the answers on a separate sheet of paper. Use a highlighter to highlight the letters that the answers have in common.

4. Based on the highlighted letters, decide which words to overlap in the puzzle. How the words overlap will determine which clues will be written across and which will be written down.

5. Complete the information on the top of the Crossword Activity Sheet. Then, write the clues in the box.

6. In the puzzle, count out how many boxes the answer to the first clue will need and outline them with a black marker. Number the clue in the first box.

7. Repeat step #6 for all of the clues.

8. Color the boxes you do not need with a marker or colored pencil.

9. Use a blank copy of the puzzle to fill in the answers to your crossword puzzle.

Note to the Teacher:
Photocopy students' puzzles so that they can make their answer sheets.

What You need:

pencil

notebook paper

highlighter

Crossword Activity Sheet

markers or colored pencils

Crossword Activity Sheet

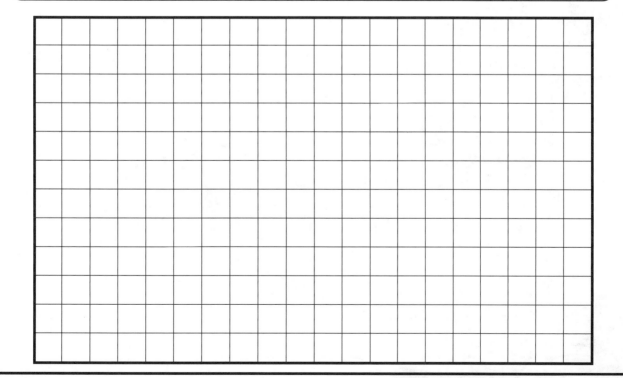

Name _____

Title _____

Author _____

Clues

Across   Down

Book Bibliography

What You Do:

1. Create a bibliography of books about a science or social studies topic after you have read a related book.

2. Complete Bibliography Activity Sheet #1. In the summary section, include important events and facts from the book.

3. Find other books about the same topic by going to a library or bookstore, or by searching the Internet.

4. Write your name and the topic of your bibliography on activity sheet #2.

5. Create the bibliography by writing the following information about each book on the sheet: book title, author's name, and a brief summary.

6. Staple the two activity sheets together.

What You need:

Bibliography Activity Sheet

pencil (or pen)

stapler

Bibliography Activity Sheet #1

Name _____

Title _____

Author _____

Summary _____

_____

_____

_____

_____

_____

_____

_____

_____

_____

_____

_____

Bibliography Activity Sheet #2

Name _____

Topic _____

Title _____
Author _____
Summary _____

_____

_____

_____

Title _____
Author _____
Summary _____

_____

_____

_____

Title _____
Author _____
Summary _____

_____

_____

_____

Title _____
Author _____
Summary _____

_____

_____

_____

sport snaps
howard balzer

Kurt Warner

the quarterback

13

This book is dedicated to my wife, Adene, and Dick Vermeil, who have always encouraged me to get in the wheelbarrow.

H.B.

PHOTO CREDITS:

David W. Preston
3, 8, 10, 20, 44, 46 left, 46 bottom, 47 left, 47 right, 48 large, 48 bottom, 49 left, 50 left, 51 right, 54, Back Cover.

Mary Butkus
1, 6, 18, 28, 30, 31, 32, 35, 36, 41, 51 left.

William Greenblatt Photography/UPI
5 left, 5 right.

The Des Moines Register
7 [G. Fandel], 22 [Bill Neibergall], 25 [Bill Neibergall].

University of Northern Iowa Public Relations Office
12.

Dan Nierling/*Waterloo Courier*
15, 16, 17.

Allsport
Front Cover [S. Halleran], 34 [B. Bahr], 38 [T. Pidgeon], 42 [B. Bahr], 43 [T. Pidgeon], 46 top [A. Bello], 48 top [B. Bahr], 49 right [A. Lyons], 50 right [E. Hasch], 52 [S. Halleran], 53 left [S. Halleran], 56 [A. Lyons].

UPI
53 right.

 © 2000 GHB Publishers, L.L.C.
All rights reserved.

Printed by Pinnacle Press, Inc. in the United States of America.

Edited by Tami Lent.

Designed by Werremeyer | Floresca.

LIBRARY OF CONGRESS CATALOG CARD NUMBER 00-101251

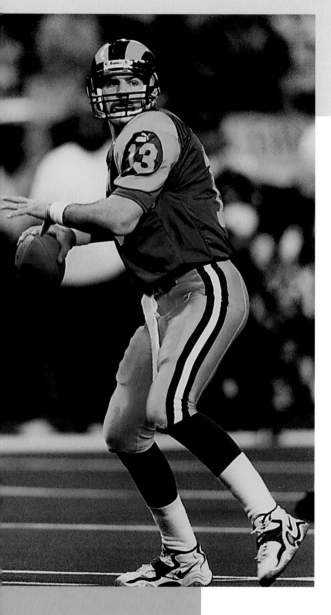

table of contents

the day

KURT WARNER WILL NEVER FORGET

He took the NFL by storm in 1999, leading the league in passing, winning every Most Valuable Player award imaginable and then guiding his team to a Super Bowl victory.

But all of that is just football, just a game. Kurt Warner will never forget the night he participated in the Billy Graham Crusade at the Trans World Dome in St. Louis on October 15, 1999.

There was a fervor among the 40,000 people in attendance when Warner walked on stage, but it wasn't only because of his ability as a football player. It was his faith that took center stage.

"I've been in this place many, many times," Warner said, "but I've never been so awestruck as I am right now. The reason is, I know you guys are not here because I can throw touchdown passes or because I can win football games. You guys are here to hear me talk about my Lord and Savior, Jesus Christ."

Warner explained that he had been "born again" about four years ago. He said, "I realized that the reason I am here is to praise and work for the man above. From that point in time, my life changed."

Warner didn't start in college until his senior season at the University of Northern Iowa, was cut after one training camp with the Green Bay Packers in 1994 and didn't get another chance in the NFL until the Rams signed him a few days after the 1997 season ended.

"But after being up here tonight and seeing what has happened the last five weeks, I realized there was a reason that the Lord brought me along the way He did," Warner said.

KURT WARNER profile

13

BORN:
JUNE 22, 1971,
BURLINGTON, IOWA

FAMILY:
WIFE, BRENDA;
CHILDREN, ZACHARY, JESSE
AND KADE

PLAYING FOR THE MINIMUM

While being the lowest-paid starting quarterback in the National Football League during the 1999 season, Kurt Warner accomplished a great many things. He made the league minimum for a second-year player—$250,000—and earned an extra $4,000 for participating in the club's off-season program.

But none of that seemed to matter to Warner, even after the Rams awarded him with a $500,000 bonus at the end of the regular season.

"Money's not something that I'm hung up with," he said. "It [the bonus] wasn't anything I went in and asked for, or anything like that. But it's obviously a nice gesture, to see that they appreciate what I've done this year."

Humble in his approach, Warner isn't that far removed from the days (after being cut by the Green Bay Packers) when he worked as a stock boy in an Iowa supermarket for $5.50 an hour. It seems hard to believe the supermarket where he once helped put cereal on the shelves now stocks Warner's Crunch Time™ cereal.

Even the proceeds from the cereal, after taxes, were being donated by Warner to Camp Barnabas, a summer camp for children with special needs.

During the season, when the subject of his contract would be brought up, Warner always answered the same way. The team and winning were always foremost on his mind.

"I don't even think about it," he said. "I came here and signed a contract. I came here to play football, and I'm playing under that contract. That's all I'm worried about right now. I'm not worried about making a lot of money. I'm worried about going out and winning football games. It just makes me laugh because I'm making a lot of money to play something that I love to play," he said.

Warner also knows that with fame and excellence, money follows, and larger contracts are on the horizon.

"Sure, I'd love a new contract at the end of the season," he said during the '99 season. "But that's not what drives me, and that's not what I'm focused on. I know that will all be taken care of in its own due time, and that somehow, some way, I'm going to prosper and be successful."

Several fund-raisers during the 1999 season in St. Louis in honor of Kurt Warner supported Camp Barnabas, a Christian summer camp in Purdy, Mo., that provides programs for children with special needs.

Warner's son, Zachary, has attended the camp. Siblings can also participate. Warner's wife, Brenda, a registered nurse, was a volunteer in the summer of 1999.

Said Brenda Warner, "These special-needs kids get to be at a camp like normal kids would be. They get to horseback ride. They get to go canoeing, all these wonderful camp things, because there is a one-on-one camper with them. And it's a Christian camp. So, they are told that God loves them, no matter what they look like, no matter what their disabilities are."

For more information on Camp Barnabas, call 417-476-2565 or go online at www.campbarnabas.com.

WHAT IS A TYPICAL EVENING AFTER A GAME LIKE? "Just relax at home with the family, order pizza, watch a movie and wrestle with Zachary."

WHAT IS YOUR FAVORITE DRINK? "Milk. And it has to be just right. I recently got a special refrigerator so it can keep the milk as cold as I like it."

WHAT WAS YOUR FAVORITE NFL TEAM GROWING UP? "The Dallas Cowboys."

KURT HELPS A YOUNG STUDENT WITH HIS SCHOOLWORK IN IOWA.

HE STANDS IN THE POCKET WITH AN EERIE CALM THAT BELIES HIS STATURE AS A FIRST-TIME STARTING NATIONAL FOOTBALL LEAGUE QUARTERBACK.

NFL | fifth-highest single-season passer rating

He deftly goes long to hit a streaking Isaac Bruce, or quickly hits Torry Holt with a slant across the middle. If none of those options are available, he ignores the chaos around him and with exceptional touch finds Marshall Faulk, the gifted safety valve.

Hardly ever does a pass touch the ground.

And when the game is over, he finds his wife, Brenda, in the stands and gives her a kiss, then tells the throng around him in the locker room that it wouldn't be possible without his faith in the Lord and the talent of his teammates.

Two days later, he is sitting in a kid's chair, pasting stars on a piece of paper during a community service visit to a center for children with visual impairment. It is something very close to the heart of this special man, whose son has been visually impaired since shortly after being born.

Understanding the phenomenon of St. Louis Rams quarterback Kurt Warner, on and off the field, requires one to go back to his strong Catholic upbringing. To say that his personality was shaped by his mother's will would be a huge understatement.

> **"I'm as happy as can be for Kurt, because I know how hard this team has worked.** I know how hard this organization has worked to put a winner on the field. They brought in new coaches, they brought in new players."
>
> TRENT GREEN, RAMS QUARTERBACK

Gene and Sue Warner moved from Burlington to Cedar Rapids, Iowa, not long after Kurt was born. Four years later, they divorced. After the split, Kurt and his brother, Matt, who is 15 months older than Kurt, lived with their mom during the week and were with their dad on weekends.

Recalled Matt, "It was difficult for both of us without having a dad there all the time. I won't say that we felt neglected or felt all that bad because we would see him a lot. But Kurt and I would hang together so much because we didn't have a full-time dad."

Sue Warner is very vocal when discussing her children. Despite the divorce, there was consistency between father and mother.

"My kids never sassed," she said. "I wouldn't tolerate it. I can't handle insolence or disrespect. I may be wrong or make a bad decision, but I am still Mom."

NFL | **second player to pass for forty touchdowns in a season (1999)**

She has no problem admitting there were times when the boys were hit in the leg with a wooden spoon to keep them in line.

Said Sue, "Tough love is hard; don't let anybody tell you it's not. But I had to be the heavy, and a lot of times I had to choose the heavy over the mom, the nice person.... Because you didn't have enough hours in the day to be both."

She worked three jobs so Matt and Kurt could attend parochial grade school and high school. Gene Warner coached some of Kurt's youth league teams. Kurt first played flag football because there wasn't enough money to play regular youth football.

Sue realized immediately that Kurt was an excellent athlete when he began playing flag football.

"He could do just about anything against older boys," she said. "He had great hands and could run better than all of them."

As for her insistence on parochial school, Sue Warner said, "It was both religious and educational. I like belief in God infiltrating into everything."

Football Tips for Young Players:
Catching the Football

KEEPING YOUR EYE ON THE BALL TO CATCH IT SEEMS LIKE SUCH A SIMPLE SKILL, BUT IT'S NOT, ESPECIALLY WHEN YOU KNOW SOMEONE IS READY TO HIT YOU IMMEDIATELY. AS A RECEIVER, FULLY EXTEND YOUR ARMS, WATCH THE BALL INTO YOUR HANDS THEN BRING IT INTO YOUR BODY. TRYING TO CATCH THE BALL AGAINST YOUR BODY WILL OFTEN RESULT IN THE BALL BOUNCING OFF YOUR PADS.

#1

At Regis High School, Kurt played football, basketball and baseball. Ninth-grade coach Jim Padlock could be credited with the decision that shaped Kurt's future. Kurt was interested in being either a wide receiver or defensive end. Becoming a quarterback was the furthest thing from his mind. But not Padlock's.

"The day he worked out for us the first time,
I was impressed by
the kind of person he was.
You could tell that he was an eager, sincere, genuine person. And there's been no change in this kid. He's still genuine. You'd have no idea that he's won all of these awards and that he's become a star."

CHARLEY ARMEY, RAMS GENERAL MANAGER

Now an assistant principal in Wilmot, Wis., Padlock remembers, "He was a good-sized kid, around 6-feet tall, and we had another kid trying out for quarterback who was very small. So we said, 'Hey, can you throw the football?'"

Kurt could and he did, but not without some trying times. Noting that he would take off and run at the slightest hint of pressure, Padlock instituted what he called the "Kill Kurt" drill. After Kurt passed the ball, two defensive linemen would knock him over, hitting him with arm pads.

Explained Padlock, "The philosophy
was to know you're going to get hit.
The other philosophy was that it hurts
a lot less when you complete the pass."

A little more than a year ago, Padlock said he saw Warner after
not talking to him for almost 10 years. Said Padlock, "The first
thing he [Warner] said was, 'Man, I hated that drill. But I learned
that you've got to just sit there and throw the ball.'"

Gaylord Hauschildt was Kurt's varsity coach in high school. Hauschildt
remarked he could see Kurt had some special gifts back then but never
anticipated the success that would come.

"He had a great arm and he could see the field like no one else who ever
played for me," he said. "But the NFL? You don't know that in high school."

Hauschildt also saw that Kurt had more than
physical ability.

"He not only knew all the plays, but he knew what everybody
else was supposed to do on each play," the coach said.
So Hauschildt decided during a game to let Kurt call the plays.
"We were in the second quarter when I turned to one of the other
assistants. Kurt had done such a good job, I asked my assistant
why shouldn't we just go home and let him handle it."

That assistant coach was Dick Breitback, who was also the Regis basketball coach. In Spring 1999, Warner attended Breitback's retirement dinner and said a few words: "There was one other goal I always had every time I played a football game in high school, and it went on to college and it goes on now. And that was to impress this man right here...I didn't ever want to let this guy down."

At the conclusion of his high school career, Kurt played for the North in the Shrine Bowl All-Star game that featured Iowa seniors. Trailing 22-15, he led his team on a touchdown drive in the final two minutes, followed by a two-point conversion that won the game.

The night before, Kurt had attended the game's banquet with longtime friend Stacy Martens. At the dinner, a speaker discussed how difficult it was to make it to the NFL.

Recalled Martens, "He told them that, at best,
two percent of them would make it."

At that point, Martens asked Kurt what he would
do without football in his life.

Said Martens, "Kurt just gave me that look he gives people when you say
something he doesn't get. Then, he said he would be in the two percent."

Even though Kurt had a successful high school career, colleges
did not line up at his door with scholarship offers.

He went to the University of Northern Iowa—and hardly played.
It got so bad, he almost quit during his junior year, his fourth year
of college. It was after a game at McNeese State that Kurt
phoned his father, as angry as he had ever been about anything.

" Here's what makes Kurt so unique: When his back is against the wall and there's pressure, that's when he plays his very best.

There's just so much to him. Poise."

MIKE MARTZ, RAMS HEAD COACH AND FORMER OFFENSIVE COORDINATOR

Said Gene Warner, "Terry Allen (UNI's coach) had promised he would play some that game and even told reporters that Kurt would get into the game. Kurt didn't see the field once. I don't think he has ever been that upset."

Kurt recalled, "I thought Coach Allen had broken his word to me. I thought I should be playing and others thought so, too."

But Gene and Sue convinced him to stay.

"I told Kurt that he was there to get an education and not to play football," Sue said. "I also told him that he had never been a quitter in his life and he shouldn't start now."

Kurt started as a senior, but got off to a shaky beginning. In his first start, ironically against McNeese State, he lost a fumble and had three passes intercepted. Northern Iowa lost 27-10. But by the time the season was over, he had passed for 2747 yards with 17 touchdowns and Northern Iowa was 6-0 in the conference, advancing to the Division I-AA semifinals.

109.2

ONE-YEAR COLLEGE STARTERS, ESPECIALLY AT SMALLER SCHOOLS, DON'T OFTEN GET NOTICED IN THE NFL DRAFT. WARNER WAS NOT SELECTED IN THE 1994 DRAFT, A YEAR IN WHICH TWO QUARTERBACKS—HEATH SHULER AND TRENT DILFER—WERE PICKED IN THE FIRST ROUND AND ONLY FIVE OTHER QUARTERBACKS WERE CHOSEN.

RAMS RECORD | single-season touchdown passes: 41

He signed a free-agent contract with the Green Bay Packers, despite the presence of Brett Favre, Mark Brunell and Ty Detmer. Warner figured as the fourth quarterback there might be more of an opportunity if there was an injury as opposed to other teams where there would be other rookies.

Admittedly overwhelmed, he was released on August 18 after only two preseason games had been played.

"I would have liked a better chance at it, but I also knew I wasn't strong enough or near ready," Warner said. "That was a very tough time for me."

A special woman helped him through the tough times. Warner, at the urging of a friend, had gone to a country music bar, where he met Brenda Meoni, four years his senior, divorced and a mother of two. One of her children, Zachary, was a special-needs child, who had been partially blinded and suffered brain damage in an accident while an infant.

Brenda had met other men who didn't come around again after hearing about her children. "I had been through that before with other guys," she said. "I figured that this was just another time."

But Kurt Warner was different.

"I really saw a lot of my mom in her," he says. "She was a strong woman who was doing the best she could in a difficult situation. She was terrific."

They began dating, despite the disapproval of Sue Warner.

NFL | sixth player to be league and Super Bowl MVP in same season

Warner remarked, "I knew she was somebody special, especially after hearing the story a little bit. I wasn't going to let anybody talk me out of it. I wasn't going to let the fact she had two kids affect me in any way. It was something that brought us together."

Meanwhile, Brenda initially wasn't thrilled with Kurt's constant comparisons of her to his mother.

"Kurt has played a lot of football from the days we had him in Green Bay. Physically, he's talented. If he continues to play the way he's playing, and there's no reason to think he won't, I think it's one of the great stories in this league this year."

MIKE HOLMGREN, SEATTLE SEAHAWKS HEAD COACH AND FORMER HEAD COACH OF THE GREEN BAY PACKERS

"I used to get really angry," Brenda said. "Now I know Sue as a strong Godly woman. I will always accept that description of myself."

After being cut by the Packers, Warner went to work at the Hy-Vee supermarket for $5.50 an hour. But his football dream never died.

"That was obviously a very humbling experience," he said. "I was making $5.50 an hour and I was darn happy to get it. I'd tell the other guys at the store, 'I'll be playing football again someday,' and they'd look at me like I was some guy who just couldn't let go."

No NFL teams called the following year, so he agreed to play Arena Football for the Iowa Barnstormers, based in Des Moines. There wasn't instant success.

Ironically, Warner's first game was an exhibition in St. Louis against the Stampede. He had two interceptions and completed only 6 of 13 passes.

Recalls Gene Warner, "I never saw Kurt so dejected. Kurt can always find something good that he did in every game. Not this one."

But he started getting better, picking up the nuances of the game, even though teammate Willis Jacox wasn't convinced.

"I didn't think there was any hope for him," Jacox said. "He couldn't get the ball to anyone quick enough and left us out there to get hammered."

But Barnstormers coach John Gregory saw something in Warner.

Said Jacox, "John kept on saying that I had to give Kurt time to develop and I wanted to get rid of him. John was right. He saw something in Kurt that no one else did."

"I'm sure he has talent, or he wouldn't be there.

The fact that he played in the Arena League doesn't have much to do with the talent he has. The guy was overlooked. That happens."

ROB BURNETT, BALTIMORE RAVENS DEFENSIVE END

It was also at that time that Warner's faith grew deeper. Brenda had become a born-again Christian, and, near the end of his first Arena season in 1995, he became born again.

"That is when I accepted that whatever happened to me, this was God's plan for me," he said. "And that I could and would accept whatever happened."

Warner's faith was put to the test in April 1996 when Brenda's parents were both killed in a tornado in Arkansas.

The Barnstormers were in training camp when Warner learned what happened. He was devastated.

Recalled Iowa kicker Mike Black, Warner's roommate, "He was crushed. He was in a hallway all by himself crying."

Said Matt Warner, "When that happened and we saw how they reacted to it, we all knew that they would be married."

But Warner's game suffered. He threw 11 interceptions in four games. He was benched at halftime in a game against Memphis after throwing two interceptions; however, he was put back in the game in the fourth quarter with Iowa trailing, 25-20, because he knew the two-minute offense the best.

There was a near interception when the defender simply dropped the ball. As time expired, Warner threw a touchdown pass to win the game.

Barnstormer Carlos James believes Warner became a leader that day.

"After that game, he seemed different, like he knew that he could win any game he played in," James said.

Kurt and Brenda were married on October 11, 1997, after Brenda began to wonder if Kurt would ever propose. She jokingly recalls a night they, along with Zach and Jesse, went out to celebrate the house they had just bought. She figured the question would come then. But it didn't.

"I was mad," she admitted. "I thought he would have proposed already."

But when they arrived home, there were four glasses ready. Two had soda and two had champagne. He asked the kids if he could marry their mom. Then, in Christmas lights on the backyard fence, the question "Will you marry me?" lit up.

Since then, their own son, Kade, was born, completing their amazing home. Kurt spends time after games watching movies and eating pizza with the kids. His home life is what's important.

After Zachary's accident, doctors told Brenda that he might not live and that he would be lucky to ever sit up.

She thought at the time, "It's up to God what becomes of him, not what the doctors tell me. He was completely blind when I took him home from the hospital. Basically, they said make it what you can. We couldn't spend a lot of time saying, 'Why Zachary? Why us? This isn't fair.' Life isn't fair. Our life proved that. It's not fair. But it all makes sense in the end."

Now 10 years old, Zachary attends a regular school, where he gets special help and is now learning to read.

The child Warner has embraced as his own amazes him.

"You could see he had accuracy. And good awareness. I think I told him last year that, personality-wise and the way he sees the field, he reminds me a little bit of Dan Fouts."

JOE PHILLIPS, MINNESOTA VIKINGS DEFENSIVE TACKLE

Football Tips for Young Players:
Tackling

YOU CAN'T TACKLE WHAT YOU CAN'T SEE. KEEP YOUR HEAD UP AND FOCUS ON THE OPPONENT'S CHEST, NOT HIS LEGS. DRIVE YOUR SHOULDERS INTO THE PLAYER, KEEP YOUR HEAD TO THE SIDE AND WRAP HIM UP FIRMLY WITH YOUR ARMS.

"He's able to do just about anything he needs to do," Warner says. "Everything might take a little longer or is more cumbersome than for other kids his age. Everything is a struggle for him. But he's an unbelievable kid and has come so far in the last few years. If you talk to him and saw him, you would never know anything is wrong.

"He's one of the most special children I ever met. He's a child who loves you for the way you love him. Whether I throw five touchdowns or five interceptions, it doesn't matter. He's got a smile on his face and is ready to wrestle with Dad no matter what. That's what life is all about.

"On the football field, I keep my emotions tied up inside. But when I'm with my family, I let them out. Zach has been such a blessing to me. He falls down, really hard, about 10 times a day, but he gets up and just exudes pure joy. He couldn't care less about football, but he touches my life so much."

There is probably no couple anywhere that is on the same wavelength as Kurt and Brenda.

"We have been through a lot of things," Kurt says. "We've had some good times and some bad times. We realize what is important in life.

"The things that are important are not throwing a bunch of touchdown passes. It's not where we hang our hat. We hang our hat on family and faith. Whether I continue to thrive on the football field, it's not what shapes who I am and who the family is. We are already the people we are and who we want to be."

After his third season in the Arena League (he threw 183 touchdown passes—including 93 in 1997—as a Barnstormer), Warner had a tryout scheduled with the Chicago Bears. While on his honeymoon, Warner suffered an insect bite on his throwing arm and the swelling caused him to miss the tryout. The Bears never called again.

nine

RAMS RECORD | single-season most 300+ yard passing games: 9

In December 1997, the Amsterdam team in NFL Europe was interested in Warner playing for them. But Warner only wanted to do it if an NFL team signed him and allocated him there. Without NFL interest, he was content playing Arena Football.

Amsterdam coach Al Luginbill talked to personnel directors with 13 (Warner's uniform number) NFL teams, including Charley Armey of the Rams.

Coincidentally, Armey's first job in coaching was at Graceville (Minn.) High School and his quarterback was Mike Kolling, who eventually was a coach at Northern Iowa.

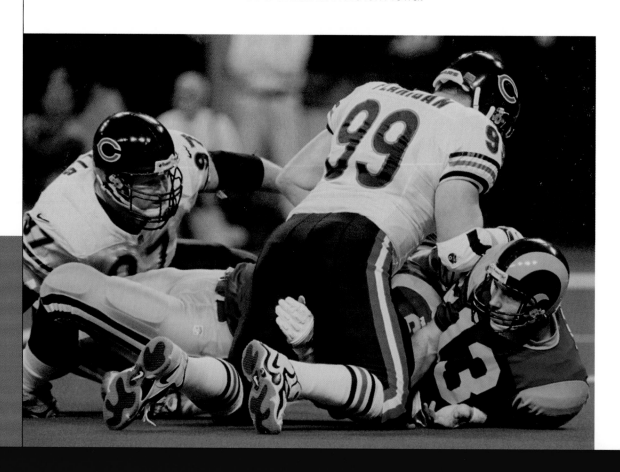

"I called Kolling to see if it would be worth a look to check out Warner, and he was very positive," Armey said. "He told us that Warner was a legitimate talent and could surprise us."

By Warner's account, he didn't believe he threw well the day of his tryout. He returned to Iowa dejected, figuring there was no way the Rams would offer a contract. But Armey saw something he liked and signed Warner to a one-year, minimum salary deal and agreed to send him to Europe.

"...It was so unbelievable," Brenda said. "But if you have the strong faith we have, anything is possible."

Warner signed with St. Louis in December 1997 (his signing was reported to the league on the day after Christmas) and he headed to Amsterdam. Married only six months before, it was not an easy time. But he needed to prove to the Rams—and himself—that he could play again on "the big field."

Warner believes all of his experiences, even if they weren't in the NFL, helped prepare him for his time with the Rams.

Said Warner, "The funny thing is a lot of people ask me what it feels like to be in the NFL playing, but it is all playing football. You still have to make reads; have to go back and make throws; you just react to what you see out there. It's the same type of thing in the Arena League that it was in college or that it is now. It is all about playing football and going out and making plays and using the ability that the Lord gave me. That is what I am doing now, but it was very valuable to me and I learned a lot.

Football Tips for
Young Players:
PASSING WITH ACCURACY

PRACTICE, PRACTICE, PRACTICE. THERE IS
NO SUBSTITUTE FOR PRACTICE. BUT YOU
HAVE TO MAKE PRACTICE PRODUCTIVE.
ALWAYS CONCENTRATE ON A TARGET,
WHETHER IT'S THROWING THROUGH A TIRE
OR AT A SPOT ON THE WALL. AND NEVER
BE SATISFIED. YOU MUST ALWAYS BELIEVE
YOU CAN DO BETTER.

"I gained confidence. Plus mentally, I was able to face a lot of different situations. I was in a lot of big games in the Arena League and as offense is [there], you have to score almost every time that you get the ball. So you build that mentality that nobody can stop you; that you go out and play football and you have to make a play every time you are out there."

Warner deeply believes the speed and quickness of the Arena game contributed to his NFL success.

"No question about it," he said. "With the dimensions smaller, you had to get back, make your reads quick and you had to be real accurate with your throws because the windows of opportunity in that league aren't very big.

"Obviously, you have some better athletes at this level, some better technicians, but you also have a lot more room to cover, a lot more distance, so some of the reads may not be quite as quick."

RAMS RECORD | single-season most passing yards: 4353

When Warner went to Amsterdam, he had to readjust to what he often called "the big field" in contrast to the 50-yard field in Arena Football.

"...You do what he's done, you're doing something well.

Aside from your natural ability, you're studying, knowing what the defense is going to do. He's the reason they're where they are right now."

ARTRELL HAWKINS, CINCINNATI BENGALS CORNERBACK

"We just call it the 50-yard indoor war," Warner said of Arena Football. "I just refer to that [the big field] because that is the biggest difference for me to go out and adjust to the different dimensions and the different size of the throws and things like that. That is why I always refer to it as the big field just because everybody says that we are always playing in a little cracker box when we are playing Arena Football."

Warner knew that having a good season in Amsterdam was important. Otherwise, the Rams probably wouldn't have taken him very seriously when training camp began. He led the Admirals to a three-way tie for first place (they didn't qualify for the playoffs because of a tie-breaker) and led the league in passing.

"It was a great experience," he said. "It was really my way to open some eyes of the people here at the Rams and around the league; that I could compete on a big field, and I could do all the things that I wasn't called upon to do in the Arena League, that you need to do on the big field.

"It just gave me a chance to reorient myself with what the large field was all about and 11-man defense. Plus, give me confidence to know that I can come into the NFL and succeed."

As Warner started to have success with the Rams, it was often said that the game seemed to slow down for him. Warner said he noticed that when he went from Arena Football to NFL Europe.

He said, "You build that clock in your head about how soon the ball needs to get off when you are playing Arena Football, so from the first couple of weeks in NFL Europe I was back there, I felt like I was standing back there with the ball for a long time; that I should just be hitting that back foot and throwing the ball. It didn't always work out that way.

"So I didn't really slow down my reads, but I had to slow down my thinking process to know that I don't have to hit that back step, that back foot and throw it every time. I realized I could get back, get set and then make the throw."

RAMS RECORD | **single-season most completions: 325**

Warner made playing in the NFL look so easy, but he knew it was not. He still had to answer questions from those who wondered if he did find it easier than his other experiences.

"I wouldn't say it's easier," he said, "because you get so many more complicated schemes and better players from top to bottom that I don't think you could ever say that this league is any easier than anything else because this is the top league and this is what it is all about. You are playing against the best, but the more you play and the more comfortable you get, I think the more a game slows down for you as a player.

Football Tips for Young Players:
BEING COACHABLE

COACHES WANT SOMEONE WHO WILL LISTEN AND RESPOND TO WHAT THEY ARE SAYING. SOMETIMES YOU MIGHT THINK THE COACH IS WRONG, BUT IF YOU GET ON THE WRONG SIDE OF YOUR COACH, NOTHING GOOD CAN COME FROM IT. ALWAYS TRY TO DO THE RIGHT THING IMMEDIATELY. COACHES LOVE PLAYERS WHO GET IT RIGHT AFTER BEING TOLD ONLY ONCE WHAT TO DO.

"And the more you can get it to slow down, the easier it is to react, the easier it is to see things. That is what the great players are able to do. They get so in tune with their surroundings and what is going on that everything seems like it is moving in slow motion. I think that only comes from playing and learning and getting comfortable with everything you see."

While Warner was in Europe, the Rams were in off-season workouts and mini-camps. He didn't attend his first Rams mini-camp until his Amsterdam season was over in June. So he needed a crash course in the Rams' offense in order to compete for a job.

RAMS RECORD | **single-season highest completion percentage: 65.1**

By the end of training camp, Warner was almost released but was retained as the No. 3 quarterback. He threw only 11 passes in a late-season loss at San Francisco. Still, no one on the Rams really knew what they had. Warner was made available to Cleveland in the expansion draft, but the Browns selected Scott Milanovich, who never made it to training camp.

"When Trent [Green] was healthy, Kurt was the whipping boy. [Mike Martz] would communicate with Trent through Kurt. Now, [third-stringer] Joe Germaine is the whipping boy. We made a conscious effort to put pressure on Kurt. I would just wear him out, but none of it fazed him."

ISAAC BRUCE, RAMS WIDE RECEIVER

The Rams signed Trent Green away from Washington and Tony Banks was traded to Baltimore.

Said Rams coach Dick Vermeil, "I told Kurt in the off-season he was my No. 2 guy. He told me, 'I won't let you down.'"

Never have truer words been spoken.

Warner played well in training camp, but Green was simply electric. Knowledgeable in the system that offensive coordinator Mike Martz brought from the Washington Redskins, Green quickly established himself as a leader. Finally, it looked like this Rams team had promise.

It all seemed to come crashing down on August 28 when San Diego safety Rodney Harrison dove into the back of Green's leg in an exhibition game, exploding Green's knee and knocking him out for the season. Green had completed all 11 of his passes to that point in the game and was 28 for 32 during the preseason.

St. Louis went into mourning, figuring another season was down the drain. Bruce pounded the turf in frustration as he knelt next to the fallen Green. Vermeil became emotional and cried briefly at a press conference the following day. Club executives openly wondered whether the franchise, then the losingest NFL team of the 1990s, was cursed.

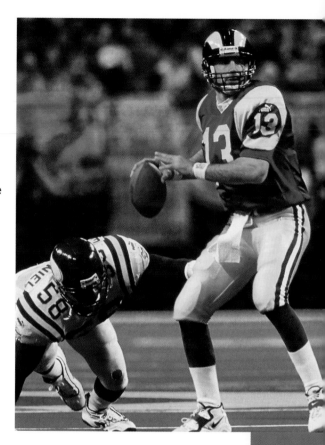

No one could have known at the time that Kurt Warner was about to make everyone quickly forget Trent Green.

Said Martz, "Kurt is just Kurt. Midway through the preseason, we felt he was still holding on to the ball a little longer then we liked. But he's also been a guy who has always responded well under pressure."

Football Tips for
Young Players:
HAVING FUN

A POSITIVE, FUN-LOVING ATTITUDE IS IMPORTANT. NO ONE WANTS TO BE AROUND SOMEONE WHO IS NEGATIVE. IF YOU'RE NOT HAVING FUN, IT MIGHT BE TIME TO FIND SOMETHING ELSE TO DO.

#6

Warner embodied the Rams' go-for-the-jugular offensive attack. Asked after the second game of the season whether it was beyond his wildest dreams to throw six touchdown passes in his first two NFL starts, he matter-of-factly replied, "I'm used to throwing eight in a game."

"Everyone was scared about our quarterback except Kurt.

Everyone was worried when Trent went down.
You could see the oxygen sucked out of the place.
The only one who never changed expression was Kurt.
Kurt Warner is Larry Bird. He has the Larry Bird look.
We lost Trent Green and they told him, 'You're our guy for the season.'
There was no batting of an eye, nothing but calm.
He just warmed up, went out and did his job."

D'MARCO FARR, RAMS DEFENSIVE TACKLE

As for finally getting his chance, Warner said, "I never had a doubt that I could play at this level. There were doubts that I'd get a chance to play here and prove it to people. But there was never any doubt in my own mind that I could do it."

He makes it look so easy, but he also realizes the talent around him has made it possible. When Warner appeared on the cover of *Sports Illustrated* after a win over the San Francisco 49ers in October 1999, he humbly wished the whole team could have been on the cover instead.

"I look back now and see all the steps that helped me get to this point and I know I could never have written that script without some help," Warner said. "It's kind of amazing, I guess."

Some would say, just meant to be.

SUPER BOWL RECORD | single-game most passing yards: 414

SUPER BOWL XXXIV CHAMPIONS

rams

WINNING
IT ALL

It still seems so improbable. The St. Louis Rams, a team that had won only 45 games in the first nine years of the 1990s, win 13 matchups during the 1999 regular season, then another three to become Super Bowl champions.

And so much of it occurred because of the golden arm of Kurt Warner, who led the NFL in passing during the regular season. He threw five touchdown passes in a playoff victory over Minnesota, a winning 30-yard score to Ricky Proehl in the NFC championship game victory over Tampa Bay and a 73-yard catch and run to Isaac Bruce that was the difference in the Super Bowl win over Tennessee.

Warner passed for 414 yards, breaking the previous Super Bowl record set by Joe Montana, and was named the game's Most Valuable Player.

Afterward, he wasn't much different than he'd been all season.

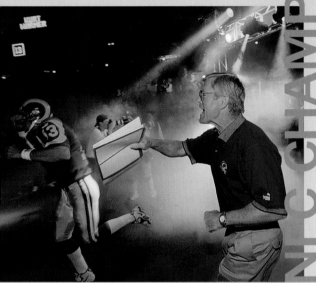

On feeling he had to play well for the team to win:

"I feel going into every game when you are the quarterback you have got to step up and you have got to play well. There is no difference in the Super Bowl. Playing against a good defense, I knew that I had to have a good game for us to win the Super Bowl. I feel that way every week. But if you are a quarterback and you don't feel like you can make the plays and don't feel like you have to make plays every week, then you are in the wrong business and the wrong position."

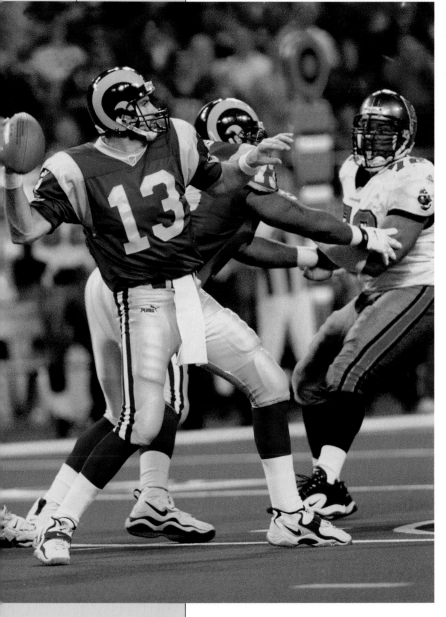

On difficulty scoring in the first half when the Rams advanced inside the Tennessee 20-yard line five times, but scored no touchdowns and led only 9-0 at halftime:

"They did a good job down there. They do a lot of combination coverages. You just have to be able to attack it; get the right guy that is one-on-one. We had a couple of shots, but they brought a lot of pressure and didn't allow me to really scan the field and find that one-on-one guy. They were bringing a lot of pressure and getting to me quickly. I had to get rid of the ball quickly down there.

"Torry [Holt] had the one that he probably could have caught. There was one at the end of the half that I had the guy [Ricky Proehl] open, but I kind of rushed my throw in the corner, otherwise we would have scored on that one. So a couple of them were things that we did to ourselves that we could have finished it. We just didn't. Then the rest of the time, you have to give them credit, they were double-teaming guys and making plays down there."

XXXIV

SUPER BOWL

On the faith of his teammates:

"The Lord has been good to me. He has blessed me. We have got a lot of great Christians on this team and we stuck together and had a lot of prayer on this team and the Lord has been faithful and He has blessed us and we are just going to give Him all the praise and glory for this one."

On never giving up:

"Just don't ever lose sight of it [your dream]. Don't let anybody tell you you can't reach it, no matter what you have to do along the way as long as you keep that dream inside of you and believe that you can accomplish it. With the Lord, all things are possible. I believe in Him and I believe in myself and with the two of us together, there is nothing that I feel we can't accomplish."

On his team believing in him:

"Everybody. The players, the coaches, Coach Vermeil. Their belief in me has been tremendous. From Day One, to just handing the job over to me, having never started in a regular season NFL game takes a lot of courage, but they obviously saw something in me that they felt that I could bring them to this level and I always knew it was in there, so I love the man [Vermeil], I love the coaches, I love everybody on this football team, and they stuck with me through this whole season. I told them from Day One that I was only going to get better and I was going to prove every one of them right. Hopefully, I have done that so far...but we will have to come out and defend now."

On being an inspiration to others:

"As I have always said, if I could be a source of hope to anybody out there, then I am happy to be a part of it. But when it is your life, you just take it day by day. You take what the good Lord gives you and you use it the best way you can, following the things that He has got in store for you. That is all I have ever done and I don't ever think of my story as a Hollywood story. It is just my life. I take it one day at a time and it has been a great year. What else can you say? It has been tremendous. I am truly blessed."

CHAMPIONS

KURT WARNER Q&A

WHAT ARE THE THINGS THAT ARE MOST IMPORTANT TO YOU?

"My **faith** and **family** are important. That keeps me on an even keel. It's a feeling that I can overcome anything; the things I have gone through with my family and adversities."

WHAT WAS THE BIGGEST ADVERSITY YOU FACED IN FOOTBALL?

"In college, it was difficult. I sat for four years and never got a chance to compete. **I wasn't given the opportunity;** I thought I should have been playing. I thought about transferring or giving up football, **but I stuck with it.**"

WHAT WAS YOUR LOWEST POINT PERSONALLY?

"**I don't like to look at it as a low point,** but it was a very difficult time when my wife's parents were killed. But it strengthened our family, and strengthened our faith and helped to bring us to the people that we are, the family that we are today."

DID YOU ALWAYS WANT TO BE A QUARTERBACK?

"Actually, **I wanted to be a receiver.** But as a freshman in high school, they needed a quarterback and the coach had us all throw the ball. I threw it the farthest so I became the quarterback. I didn't want to make the switch, but I'm glad I did. I like the control, the ball in my hands. I know where the ball is going to go; it's up to me to win or lose."

DO YOU REMEMBER REFUSING TO GO INTO A SCRIMMAGE IN TRAINING CAMP WITH THE PACKERS?

"I don't remember that. I've read about that and I honestly don't remember it. Maybe I pushed it out of my mind. But I guess it probably did happen and assuming it did, I was probably overwhelmed so I didn't want to go in and screw up."

WHAT IS YOUR FAVORITE PASS?

"The intermediate throws. Sure, it's nice hitting a long bomb. But I like to keep moving the football methodically. I like those types of situations. In the red zone or third down when the pressure is on."

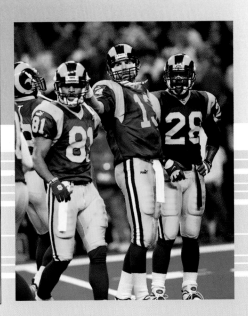

IT SEEMS YOU'VE ALWAYS BEEN A WINNER. IS THAT TRUE?

"Everywhere I've been I've won football games. Things have happened when I've played."

WHAT ABOUT YOUR PERSPECTIVE?

"It doesn't allow me to go up and down on the football field, but it's allowed me to keep an even keel to know that no matter what happens on the football field that it's not ever going to affect me. Not that it's not going to upset me if I lose or I don't play well, but I'm not going to let it affect the kind of person that I am and the way I carry myself off the field. My faith and my family are so much more important than that and can help me overcome anything that happens on the football field."

Throughout the 1999 off-season, the Rams' organization struggled with the decision of whether to sign a veteran backup to Trent Green. Green had been signed as a free agent to be the team's starting quarterback, and, with the departure of Steve Bono, the only quarterback on the roster was the untested Kurt Warner.

While various options were considered, then-coach Dick Vermeil opted to stick with Warner as the backup. That choice was supported by Mike Martz, hired as the team's new offensive coordinator, who, after arriving in St. Louis, was immediately impressed by Warner's demeanor and work ethic.

Vermeil explains what made Warner able to excel when no one expected it.

Vermeil on Warner emerging from obscurity:

"There are a lot of quarterbacks who have been first-round picks that have been given all the opportunities, all the coaching, all the money, all the everything, and they are on their third team and they are still going to fail. This kid...you talk about coming from nowhere and sticking with it and staying with it. He had nothing going for him except good character. It's just so exciting to see a guy just come up from nowhere."

Vermeil on how his own confidence grew in Warner as the season progressed:

"I always had confidence in him. Now I have blind confidence in him. Gosh, when he throws an incomplete pass, I'm saying 'What's wrong with you?' I told him this morning, 'I don't know how long this can keep going, but I'm enjoying it.'"

Vermeil on Warner's gift:

"Maybe his greatest asset is that he's oblivious to the pass rush. When he's in the pocket, he doesn't break his concentration. I don't know if you can coach that. It's just the way you are.

"He spoils you. There were those who wondered if he could keep it up. This is obviously what he is. He is gifted. Whether it was Arena or World League, those were the most important games to him at the time. He used those games to improve."

Other quotes from Dick Vermeil:

"A lot of young quarterbacks struggle to adjust to the speed of the game. That's something you can't glean from watching them practice. This kid slows the game down a little bit, and part of that's because of what he went through in the Arena League."

"I'm extremely happy for Kurt. I'm a lunch-pail guy. I really get more excited about seeing that kind of thing happen than I do seeing your first-round pick go to the Super Bowl."

Before the season started:

"Kurt Warner has never been given a good enough opportunity. Well, he has earned the one he has here. I stuck my neck out on him, and I believe he will do a fine job."

Famous last words

Dick Vermeil had this to say on September 12, 1999, after Kurt Warner had led the Rams to a season-opening 27-10 victory over the Baltimore Ravens: "I've been around this game a long time. I've coached quarterbacks most of my career, and I have a pretty good feel for them. I think this guy is a good football player. Hey, he ain't going to the Pro Bowl right now. But we can win with Kurt Warner."

Well, one out of two isn't bad.

ABOUT DICK VERMEIL

DICK VERMEIL HAS BEEN A WINNER WHEREVER HE HAS COACHED. WHETHER IT WAS IN HIGH SCHOOL, COLLEGE OR THE NFL, VERMEIL'S UNIQUE BRAND OF MOTIVATION RESULTED IN HIGH ACHIEVEMENT FOR HIS TEAMS.

IN 1976, HE TOOK OVER THE DOWNTRODDEN PHILADELPHIA EAGLES. IN FIVE SEASONS, THE EAGLES WERE IN THE SUPER BOWL. CITING BURNOUT, VERMEIL RETIRED AFTER THE 1982 SEASON AND WAS OUT OF COACHING FOR 14 YEARS UNTIL TAKING THE REINS OF THE ST. LOUIS RAMS IN 1997.

AFTER TWO DISMAL SEASONS AND A COMBINED 9-23 RECORD, VERMEIL BECAME THE FIRST COACH EVER TO LEAD HIS TEAM FROM LAST PLACE IN THEIR DIVISION TO A SUPER BOWL TITLE.

FAITH AND THE WHEELBARROW

During every Rams practice, a blue wheelbarrow sat on the side of the practice field. It reminded players of a message in their playbooks, one that Kurt Warner certainly embodied.

The message told the story of a man who traveled from one small town to another, performing a tightrope act. One day, he came to a little farming community. He stood in the center of the town square and announced that he was going to go to the outskirts of town, stretch a rope across the wide river canyon and walk across the rope while pushing a wheelbarrow.

Naturally, the farmers were skeptical. They didn't think he could do it. So the man went to the edge of town, put his rope between two trees about five feet off the ground and began to practice. He got up on the rope with his wheelbarrow and walked back and forth, back and forth.

One farmer came out and began to watch. And the longer the farmer watched, the more he became convinced that the man could do what he said he was going to do. So, the farmer went back to the town square, where the skeptics were, and said, "Do you all remember that man who said he was going to walk a tightrope across that wide canyon? Well, I believe he can do it."

The skeptics laughed uncontrollably. "No he can't," they all said.

The believing farmer said, "Well, come on out to the edge of town. I want you all to watch him."

And they all went out to where the man was practicing on the rope. The one farmer said, "See, he's doing it. I told you he could do it."

The non-believers laughed again and said, "Yeah, but that rope is only five feet off the ground. It's not hundreds of feet in the air across that big canyon."

And the believer said, "Well, I'll tell you how much I believe. I'll bet you $10 he can do it."

And when he said that, the man on the rope stopped, turned in his direction and said, "Do you believe I can walk across that wide canyon on this rope while pushing a wheelbarrow?"

The farmer replied, "I sure do. I bet $10 on you, didn't I?"

And the man on the rope said, "O.K., get in the wheelbarrow!"

As it is said, it's one thing to stand on the sideline and say, "I believe." It's quite another to get in the wheelbarrow.

Without a shred of doubt, Kurt Warner certainly got in the wheelbarrow.

"My goodness,
what a story
this is."

TALK-SHOW HOST DAVID LETTERMAN